PIECES OF MUSIC

ROBERT BRINGHURST

PIECES OF MAP,

PIECES OF MUSIC

謝琰題字

with calligraphy by

Yim Tse

COPPER CANYON PRESS

ISBN 978-1-55659-003-0

First published in Canada by McClelland and Stewart, Limited, in 1987. First U.S. edition by Copper Canyon Press published in 1987.

The publication of this book is made possible by a grant from the National Endowment for the Arts.

Copper Canyon Press is in residence with Centrum at Fort Worden State Park.

Typography by Robert Bringhurst; composition by The Typeworks, Vancouver. The face is Aldus, designed by Hermann Zapf. The cover is a wall relief from the tomb of Patenemheb, Dynasty XVIII.

COPPER CANYON PRESS
P.O. Box 271, Port Townsend, WA 98368

ᓂᑐᒪᓪ ᑲᕐ ᑐᑭᓄᐊᓕᖃᒪᓪ

ᓂᑐᒪᑲᒃ ᓄᐢᑕ ᑲᑭᕐᑭᓄᐊᓕᖏᒃ ᐅᒥ

CONTENTS

THE BOOK OF SILENCES

The Jain teacher Parśvanatha was, or may have been, a contemporary of Homer. The Zen master Hakuin, born in 1685, was three years older than Alexander Pope, though he sounds more like Herakleitos. This sequence of brief impersonations begins in India with the one and concludes in Japan with the other. The speakers between are the ghosts of other thinkers and singers, most of them from China, most of them students of the Tao and of the Buddhadharma.

In the midst of an empire as arrogant, ethnocentric, greedy and corrupt as the North American empire at present, the sages of Tang Dynasty China practised and preached a tradition of freedom both from the pride of imperial service and from the anesthesis of complicity. Like the Presocratics, they reached toward the joints and roots of poetry and thinking. Most of them were wanderers, and most of them resettled, taking new names from the neighboring mountains. They are not just people who were places; they are people who *became* places − when everything encouraged them instead to become consumers and provisioners: bureaucrats or managers; trapped, co-opted laborers or lords.

Ξυνόν ἐστι πᾶσι τὸ φρονέειν, says Herakleitos: *All things think,* or *thinking is the thing that links all things.*

I want a poetry of knowledge and of thought, not of opinion − and not of belief, which is merely dead thought, severed from the thinking. Poetry is the musical density of being, but sometimes it is *silent,* and sometimes that silence is musically still. Those whom I hoped to make speak here spoke for its sake. For themselves, they mostly listened.

From the mouth came speech, from speech fire. A nose appeared; from the nose came breath, from breath the air. The eyes appeared; from the eyes came sight, and from sight the sun. The ears appeared; from the ears came hearing; from hearing, the four quarters. The skin appeared; from the skin came hair, from hair vegetation. The heart appeared; from the heart came the mind, from the mind the moon. So at any rate it is claimed in the Aitareya Upanishad.

What is whole has no face. What
is apart from the whole has no body.

Yet somehow it is, and it is
manysided. Somehow it isn't
and is manysided. Somehow
it is manysided and isn't
and is. It cannot be touched
by the mind or by language, but somehow,
in spite of our thinking and talking,
it is, and in spite of our thinking
and talking, it isn't. Beyond
all our thinking and talking,
it isn't and is. This
is a map of our knowing. Own
nothing. Like breath in your lungs,
the truth passes through you.
Where space, motion and rest
come together is being. Where being
is tainted by death, you find
matter. Like water through cloth,
the unbroken plasma of action
drains through your bones.
What you are will be spelled by whatever
lies trapped in your hand.

On the fenceposts the heads of your
hungerless brothers are singing.

UDDALAKA ARUNI:
A SONG FOR THE WEAVERS

Earth is woven of water, as water
of air. The world is earth, and the earth
is all this. This is that. That is you,
Śvetaketu, my son. The outer is inner.

The sea has no end, in spite of its edges.
The seed is the tree's thought. The seed
is the speech of the tree. The seed is the tree
thinking and speaking its knowledge of trees.

The mind is the white of the egg in its opening
shell, the mind is the ripening
meat of the seed. Out. In. Out. In. What is
is the weaving. We with our breathing

are working here, carding and spinning the air.

般若波羅蜜多

What is is swollen like a ripe
fruit, hollow like a cave.
What you touch, hear, taste, see, smell
is the inner perfection of vision.

What reaches into our eyes and our ears
is what is, and that is the wordless, inaudible
song and the brooding, unmusical
speech of the world.

This too
is just one
more opinion
to move through.

What is is what lies
out of sight, thought and talking.
Open them. Open the three
fists clinging to the world.

Open this too.
All positions
are prisons.
No truth is true.

No instruction is certain, no knowledge complete.
If I speak for the serpent, the serpent
may speak for the bird. My position
is that I have no position.

This too.
All fictions
are true.
All intentions,

positions,
and all dispositions
are prisons;
this too.

What is has no essence.
What is is interdependent and empty.
What is is unsingle, undouble, unplural, unborn,
unenduring, unbearing, undying;

what is has no past and no future, no shape
and no nature, no being, no having been, going
to be or becoming, no wholeness and no
incompleteness, no fingers. . . .

This too.
This too
is just one
more opinion.

Outside the perfection of light there is no
total darkness. What causes what is is the hunger
to be and keep being. What is is on loan
from what isn't and is its reflection.

*What is is on loan from what isn't and is
its disguise.* There is no rock bottom.
No centre, no sides, no top and no bottom.
This too.

There are no literal statements.
There is no unmetaphorical language.
This too.
Emptiness also is empty.

Nothing is not nothing. Nothing
is, and *is* is nothing. All that is
is nothing, yet there is
no nothing there that we can cling to.

*We are also then
the nothing,*
and the nothing
is the hunger,

*and the hunger
is the question*
and the answer:
be pure wonder.

天地うし心

Wáng Bì of Wei
lies dead in his hut
at age 24. His mind
is now one with the mountain.
His flesh has been grass,
voles, owls,
owl pellets, grass.

The use of the is
is to point to the isn't.
Go back, said Wáng Bì:
Look again at the mind
of the sky and the heart
of the mountain. The mind
is unbeing. The mind
of heaven and earth
is unbeing. Go back,
look again. What is,
is. It consists
of what isn't. *Are*
is the plural of *is*; *is*
is the plural of *isn't*. Go back,
look again. What isn't,
is. This
is the fusion of substance
and function, the heart of the sky
and the mind of the mountain.

To be, said Wáng Bì,
without being: this
is the way to have virtue.
Don't fondle it, stand
on what isn't. We sink, said Wáng Bì,
when we set out to stand on what is.

聖心冥寂

SENGZHAÒ

The thought of the gods is dark water. The gods
have their destinies too as they move through the world.
Our speech does not reach them. As for our speechlessness,
what shall we say? And to whom shall we say it?
What is is not easy and graceful to speak of.
My teacher, a foreigner, lame in the tongue
like a caged raven, knew this.
I, however, was born here. Forgive me,
that sometimes I sink into elegant phrase.

The gods' minds and their mindprints are one
in the same. With us it is different. Our footprints
fall off as we walk through the world. Our brilliant
assertions tack like October leaves
through the air before mouldering. Yes and no
are at home in each other, not elsewhere. What is
and who knows of its presence are one in the same.

The feet are the link
between earth and the body. Begin there.
The lungs are the link between body and air.
The hands, these uprooted feet, are the means
of our shaping and grasping. Clasp them.
The eyes are the hands of the head;
its feet are the ears.

We are all of us here in the hidden
house of the unnamed. You
who insist we must visit
and name it have ceased to be there.

BODHIDHARMA

I cut off my eyelids,
he cut off his arm.
He could not hold the cleaver
to cut off the other.

He could have kept both
had he noticed this sooner.
The scars of our errors
are taken for signs.

There is no other side
to this wall, though the road
is so wide it leads through.
It leads through. That is all.

I can affirm
that there is nothing to affirm
and there is nothing to deny.
What neither is nor isn't is
what is. It is
unthinkable, unspoken. So
we speak of it as ultimate
and ordinary, absolute,
routine. And this
two-sidedness
is its function.

物我同根

What is
is what isn't. What isn't
is water. The mind is a deer.
In the lakes of its eyes,
the deer and the water
must drink one another.
There are no others,
and there are no selves.
What the water sees
is — and is not what you think
you have seen in the water.

There is no something, no nothing,
but neither. No is
and no isn't, but neither. Now,
don't defile the thought
by sitting there thinking.
No difference exists
between body and mind, language
and mind, language and body.
What is, is not. You must love,
and let loose of, the world.

I used to write poems,
and like yours, they were made
out of words, which is why
they said nothing.
My friend, there is only one word
that I know now, and I have somehow
forgotten its name.

What is the brain but the back of the face?
Climb down from the elephant
of the mind you are riding, climb down
and leave it to drink
or to drown in the river.

What stirs in the heart
comes to rest in the heart
like dust in a cave.

Thought is thought, and not
anything more. Seeing is seeing.
What is is what is. These three together
are what they are, and their total is one,
which is what there is and is equal
to zero. A is not A; one is not one;
this too is the rule.

Only insofar as one is
speechless can one really
think with words.

The mind appears to be
because of what the mind
appears to think of.
Nothing is external. Only

knowing is external. Only
knowing is beyond the reach
of knowing. Pure unbeing
is a seamless understanding of the world.

When it is known that there is
no such thing as knowing,
thought that no such thing as thinking
is, then thinking comes to pass.

In all of what is, there is
nothing quite lifeless.
No one who falls can rise
without help from the ground.

The ground is external.
What is is what you cannot
carry with you and what can't
be left behind.

Friends, the mind, or at any rate
my mind at this moment, is much
like the moon. It is swollen
with light, it is dry and in motion.

Its taste and its smell, its feel
in the skull, are as those of the moon
over the steep hills and the bottomless
pools of deep autumn.

Friends, what is is much like the pool.
What is not is not unlike the air,
and what neither is nor is not neither is
nor is not like or unlike the hills.

This being so, there is no
comparison, is no description, assertion,
negation. I tell you conclusively,
there can be no conclusions.

I am leaving now. Please,
no applause. Those who know how to live
will leave with me
in different directions.

I

Take no shit, said Línjì.
Behead the Buddhas. Cow the pig of the world.

Take hold of it, use it, but do not
give it a name: this is the ultimate principle.

Sleep, eat, pee:
this is the essence of the way.

Build a boat in the mountains,
a ferry at sea,

but no speculation, no fortification, no bridges,
burned or unburned.

There is nothing to do. The answer
is perched on your lips like a bird.

If it nests in your mouth, how will you speak?
How will you weave if it nests in your hands?

Singing and dancing! These are the signs
of the silent and still.

Is? No. Isn't? No. Is and isn't? Neither is nor isn't?
No! No! None of these and more.

Host and guest, we eat one another
for breakfast. This too is the way.

What you see in the eyes of the deer as it wheels
and flees is not terror but horror.

Only a man with no hands
can reorder the world.

II

To hear in the chirp of the bird the original
isn't, and in the answering chirp of the bird
that what is is what isn't and this is
the whole of the dusty world
is to die a good death,
trampled by watersnakes, torn
on the antlers of the snowshoe hare.

There is nowhere to go. Nothing
is *there*. What is
is all *here*, and what isn't
is everywhere.

You can begin by renouncing
your home, if you are so brash as to think
that you have one. Know this: the true face
has no features, the true man no name
and of course no address.

Dying is one more simple thing everyone does,
like scratching the ear and undressing.

Thought and not thinking
are one. Is and isn't
are one. Sword, swordsman, stroke
and not striking are one. One and not one
are one. One is not two. One is also
not one. This arithmetic
lives in the flowering
heart of the world.

一箭過青天

Let me tell you a story. The gardener
and the cook sat together
in the garden. A jay sang. The gardener

tapped his fingernails against
his wooden chair. A jay sang
again. The gardener tapped

his chair again. A jay
did not sing. The gardener,
for the third time, tapped

his wooden chair. The cook was sitting
quietly, while all this
was happening, sipping his tea.

The whole earth closes
like a fist and touches,
once, the rimless drum,

and slowly opens
like a rose
while no one listens.

The skull on the hill
wakes from its dream
before morning.

Impeccably dressed
though it is
in moonlight and moss,

and well fed, and well
rested, it gives
not a thought to returning.

心地乾淨方可

讀書學古

Stone under plum and bamboo,
their conjunction. Like them
to be artless, not thoughtless,
all the way through. I have read
many books, and now
cannot write one. They too.

Longheartedness, that
is the answer. The wind
is a short flute, but the heart
is long. Longheartedness, yes,
but what is has no size. As its measure,
which flute shall we use?

When the face of a man is as thin
as a pine, his joy and his grief do not leak
through his eyebrows. Where is the right,
where is the wrong in the slow
wooden fountain we know as bamboo? Is a species
a law enforced by the court, or is it an idea?

Or is it unbeing folded through being, a sudden
reflection, an image, a vision
through which other images, other visions
are tumbling and spilling? A vision
to which other visions are constantly
fed, and on which they are feeding?

Craneflies in autumn, finches in spring
cherish their natures.
A waste of the mind to parcel what is

into ugly and beautiful. Useless
to fall for the habit of happy and sad.
A man may hold present and past

like two frightened thrushes
alive in his fists while another
holds nothing. Sooner or later
each must release what he has.
All that isn't, sooner or later,
must sweep through their hands.

But you who retreat into solitude do it
to fondle the self and say *ahhh*.
Water and rock
are the roots of right action.
Bathe in the spaces. Here you are merely
sweeping the stream.

How much of the mind is confined to the body?
Conversely, how much of the memory rests
in the earth, and how much of the mind
in what the mind touches: the stars and the clouds,
the color and shape of the woodpecker's
crest, and the web of his motion?

So you can read
a book full of words.
Can you read one without words?
You can bring music
out of that lute after tuning
the strings. Can you play one without strings?

One man listens to music
or looks at a painting
and nurtures his mind with them.
Another wants from them only
their physical energy.
One walks the mountains

and studies the clouds to draw wisdom
and strength from them.
To another, they are loud noises
in visible terms. They may frighten
or thrill him, but what
does it matter? What has he learned?

Taste the still air,
hear the still water: new leaves
will spring from the doorpost.
Plum and bamboo will rise through you.
Snowflakes and stones will set roots
through your shoulders and hands.

音心似秋月

Wind through the warp
of the waterfall, talking.
Moon above the hill across the harbor,
climbing and gleaming.

When I am dead and my bones lie
mindlessly in the dirt,
they will be
as transparent as ever.

All beings are gods. Gods
are all beings. The ice on the river
is time in the grip of your mind
in the grip of the water. What is
has no future, no present, no past,
no place and no nature. The knowledge of this
has likewise no nature.
Cause and effect are the same:
there is not even one.
Still less is there neither.

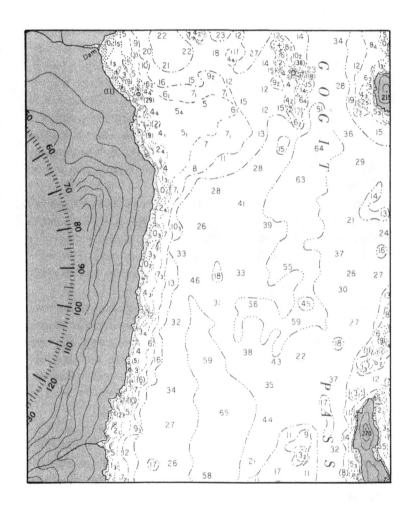

The archipelago of Haida Gwai lies like a forested, rain-drenched Cyclades in a corner of the North Pacific. Like the Cyclades, it holds somewhere within itself – as anyone can tell by simply listening – one centre of the world. On all the maps, it is shown off the coast of Alaska and British Columbia under the impudent, uninquisitive name which a British sailor elected to give it in 1787: the Queen Charlotte Islands.

Lyell Island is one of this intricate chain. It was partially logged when I saw it first, in the 1970s. When I saw it again, the fallers had reached the trees near the murrelet breeding grounds. Thousands of birds, just in from their winter at sea, drifted homelessly in the bay, away from the noise of the saws and the yarders. In 1985, a few native islanders – the Haida of Haida Gwai, who wanted the fish, the deer, the bear, and the rest of the living culture the trees sustain – confronted the white colonial government wanting the cashflow it saw in the logs. Much talk ensued about the dollar value of tourism versus the dollar value of logs – as if, when the values in question exceeded not only our culture's but our species' bounds, the answer could still be written in dollars.

On the east side of the island is the old site of Hlqia, or Goshawk Town, at Windy Bay. Just off lies Gogit Passage. The name means Madman's Passage, from the Haida *gagiit*, a lunatic or outlaw: one outside the reach of culture: one who can't, or won't, remember what things mean, and what one can and what one can't afford to kill where one intends to go on living.

Where the trees remain is that strangely depopulated richness we like to call wilderness: a world from which the humans who knew it were skimmed by the epidemics of smallpox and religiosity that reached these islands in the 1830s. Where the trees are gone, the slash rots, the rain washes loam back to bedrock, and lichens are starting. With lichens – algae enslaved and domesticated by fungi – the recolonization begins.

In the meantime, much washes up on the beaches, changed by the journey. Dislodged bits of the world wash up on the beaches, pickled and dead, or seachanged into something rich yet skeletal, familiar and yet strange. Like these small offerings from elsewhere, gathered in the shadow of the island's momentary name.

In another time, stories and songs were transformed as they passed through the prism of languages on this coast. They rotated and changed as they moved through the Salishan into the Wakashan tongues, and from Tsimshian and Haida to Tlingit and Tahltan and back again. This is an album of mere mistranslations, or it is a cycle of songs which have altered, as might have seemed right to men and women whose flesh is now trees — and of whom we should think as the trees are falling.

... es sind / noch Lieder zu singen jenseits / der Menschen
– Paul Celan

In the threadbare
air, through the tattered
weave of leaves,
the blue light cools
into ash-black shadow.

Tree: the high
thought roots itself
in the luminous clay
of the caught light's closeness
to audibility.

So we know that again
today, there are songs
still to be sung. They
exist. Just on the other
side of mankind.

. . . et la terre mauvaise dans le champ de son coeur
— René Char

Once upon a time there was a man
who never hungered anymore,
or so I heard — he had devoured so many legacies,
bitten off anything, eaten through anyone who came near —

who one day found
that his table was cleared,
his bed emptied, his children renamed,
and the soil gone sour in the uplands of his heart.

He had dug no grave; he had thought to survive.
He had nothing to give; he had less to receive.
Objects avoided him, animals lied to him,
the Diamond Sutra hung, untranslatable, on his wall.

It was only then that he crept back in
and stole hunger and shaped it into
a bowl, in which, to this day, when no one
is looking, and the wind not blowing, he bathes.

Douceur d'être et de n'être pas
— Paul Valéry

Her footfalls, born of his voicelessness,
paving their way, like a saint's steps, patiently
lead, windchilled and mute,
toward the watchman's bed.

Shoeless like the gods, and the long light
laid across her arms.
All the words, all the silences disguised as words,
adrift between us and the unsaid.

Finally her lips close in, the invisible
nutrition of the kiss
opening the dark bouquet of mouths
wadded into his head.

Take your time. He has always been there
waiting, and his heart out stalking, still
when you are still and moving as you move,
matching your stride, echoing your tread.

... der da mit seinem Schatten / getränktes liest
– Rainer Maria Rilke

Who reads her while she reads? Her eyes slide
under the paper, into another world
while all we hear of it
or see is the slow surf of turning pages.

Her mother might not recognize her,
soaked to the skin as she is in her own shadow.
How could you then? You with your watch and tongue
still running, tell me: how much does she lose

when she looks up? When she lifts
the ladles of her eyes, how much
flows back into the book, and how much
spills down the walls of the overflowing world?

Children, playing alone, will sometimes
come back suddenly, seeing what it is
to be here, and their eyes are altered. Hers too. Words
she's never said reshape her lips forever.

Miesiąc jak królik wśród obłoków hyca
– Jarosław Iwaszkiewicz

The moon sneaks like a rabbit from cloud to cloud.
In the darkness you can't see the funerals.
The light – no matter how little or much
we are given – spills down our cheeks,
though a portion is eaten each day
by our eyes, to feed the inedible
fruits of our voices.

Nevertheless, that moon up there
scares me. It's priestly. I think it may
visit me someday, any day, shaped
like a boy.

The gods and the stars are all flying away.
Does anyone still think anything really
remains here? You're leaving too, I guess,
are you? Already?

Listen in simple words
to what I say. I know I sometimes
speak it – like an educated
foreigner – a little too
clearly. Even so, it is
your own tongue: which no one
anywhere may ever speak to you again.

Parfois l'air se contracte / Jusqu'à prendre figure.
— Jules Supervielle

Ravenous giraffes, you
star-lickers, steers
seeking the infinite in
a movement of the grass,

greyhounds out to catch it
on the run, roots
who know that it is
hidden down there somewhere:

what has it turned into
in me now that I am no more
than alive and all my handholds
are transparent sand?

The air contracts like something
taking form, but there is nothing
one can't kill if one is willing
to keep moving. Earthly

recollections, tell me
how to speak
with trees, with sea-waves
breaking, with a sleeping child. This

is what I wanted: just
to pacify my longfaced
memory, to tell it
a more patient story.

debo reanudar mis huesos en tu reino
— Pablo Neruda

A man with no hands is still singing.
A bird with no hands is asking the world,
and the world is answering every day:
earth is the only flesh of the song.

A man with no wings is crossing
the sky's black rapids on his hands.
His mother's bones lie slumped
by the stumps of the cedars.

I carry my own bones in my hands
into your country,
and there are no kings; it is not a kingdom;
and there is no legend; it is the land
and a woman's body, and these are my bones.
What do I owe to these strangers my brothers?

GIFTS & PRESENCES

Ce dire *et ce* se dédire *peuvent-ils*
se rassembler, peuvent-ils être en même temps?

Can this *saying* and this *being unsaid* be
assembled? Can they be at the same time?

— EMMANUEL LEVINAS
Autrement qu'être ou au-delà de l'essence

The heart is a white mountain
left of centre in the world.
The heart is dust. The heart is trees.
The heart is snowbound broken
rock in the locked ribs of a man
in the sun on the shore of the sea who is dreaming
sun on the snow, dreaming snow on the broken
rock, dreaming wind, dreaming winter.

The heart is a house with torn floorboards.
The heart is a seeded and peeled
grape on the vine, a bell
full of darkness and anvils.
The heart is a flute with four fingerholes
played in the rain.
The heart is a deep well dug upward.

The heart is a sandstone canyon in the high
Triassic fields, inhabited by grass,
potsherds and scapulae, femurs and burnt corn,
with horned men and mountain sheep
painted and pecked in the straw-colored walls.

The heart is three bowls
always full and one empty.
The heart is a four-winged
bird as it lifts and unfolds.
The heart is a full set of goatprints,
a pocket of unfired clay and a stray
piece of oatgrass:
two fossils: one locket;

a drenched bird squawking from the perch
in its overstuffed cage.

The heart is a deep-water sponge
tied up with smooth muscle in two
double half-hitches, sopping up blood
and twice every second wrung out like a rag.

The heart is a grave
waking, a corpse walking, a tomb
like a winter well-house, pulsing
with blood under the wilted noise
of the voices. The heart is a cut root
brooding in the worn earth,
limping, when no one is watching,
back into the ground.

The heart is four hands serving soup
made of live meat and water.
The heart is a place. The heart is a name.

The heart is everything, but nothing
is the heart. The heart is lime and dung and diapers
in a hole. The heart is wood. The heart is
diamond and cooked turnip, lead and precious metal,
stone. The heart is light. The heart is cold.

The heart is a smoking saxophone rolled
like a brass cigar in a mouth
like the mouth of Ben Webster,
something perforated, folded,
always emptying and filling,
something linking aching air
and a wet, shaking reed.

The heart is four unintersecting
strokes of the brush in Chinese,

with these homophones:
daylight, zinc, firewood, bitterness, joy,
earthbreath and *lampwicking,*
up which the blood is continually rising.

The heart is a pitcher of untasted water.

The heart is a white mountain
which the woman in the moon,
her left breast full of cellos and her right
breast full of violins,
climbs and is sometimes carried
up and down.

The heart is found
in the leaking bucket of the ribs,
in the distant hills, in the lover's
body, the belly, the mouth,
in the empty wheel between the knees.

The heart is being
knowing only that it is;
the heart is dumb; the heart is glass.

The heart is dust
trees locket rock sponge
white mountain peeled stone
house flute bell rain

The heart is being aching, being
beating, being knowing being
that not what not
who not how not why
it is the beating that it is.

Knowing, not owning.
Praise of what is,
not of what flatters us
into mere pleasure.

Earth speaking earth,
singing water and air,
audible everywhere
there is no one to listen.

RUBUS URSINUS:
A PRAYER FOR THE BLACKBERRY HARVEST

Reaching through thorns,
milking the black
udders with stung
wrists. Sister and
mother and un-
named stranger, say:
whose is this dark
blood on my hands?

for Don McKay & Jan Zwicky

Moonset at sunrise, the mind
dividing between them. The teeth
of the young sun sink through the breast of the cloud.
And a great white pelican rests in the bay,
on his way from Great Slave Lake
to Guatemala.
The mind is made out of the animals
it has attended.
In all the unspoken languages,
it is their names.

To know is to hold no opinions: to know
meaning thinks, thinking means.
The mind is the place not already taken.
The mind is not-yet-gathered beads of water
in the teeth of certain leaves –
Saxifraga punctata, close by the stream
under the ridge leading south to Mount Hozameen,
for example – and the changing answers of the moon.
The mind is light rain gathered
on the ice-scarred rock, a crumpled mirror.

To be is to speak with the bristlecone
pines and the whitebarks,
glaciers and rivers, grasses and schists,
and if it is permitted, once also
with pelicans. Being
is what there is room for in that
conversation. The loved is what stays
in the mind; that is, it has meaning,

and meaning keeps going. This
is the definition of meaning.

What is is not speech.
What is is the line
between the unspeakable
and the already spoken.

FOR THE BONES OF JOSEF MENGELE, DISINTERRED JUNE 1985

Master of Auschwitz, angel of death,
murderer, deep in Brazil they are breaking
your bones – or somebody's bones: my
bones, your bones, his bones, whose
bones does not matter. Deep in Brazil they are breaking
bones like loaves of old bread. The angel
of death is not drowning but eating.

Speak! they are saying. *Speak! speak!*
If you don't speak we will open and read you!
Something you too might have said in your time.
Are these bones guilty? they say. And the bones
are already talking. The bones, with guns
to their heads, are already saying, *Yes!*
Yes! It is true, we are guilty!

Butcher, baker, lampshade and candlestick
maker: yes, it is true. But the bones? The bones,
earth, metals, teeth, the body?
These are not guilty. The minds of the dead
are not to be found in the bones of the dead.
The minds of the dead are not anywhere to be found,
outside the minds of the living.

TENDING THE FIRE

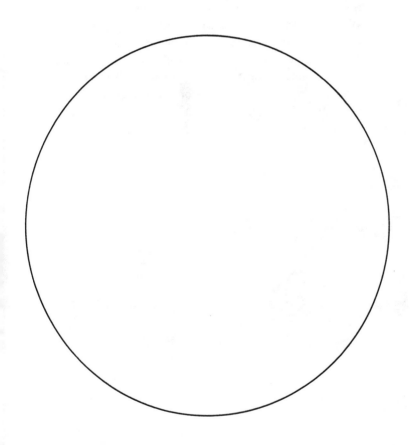

This story belongs to Ron Evans of Saskatchewan and to Jesús Elciaga of Oaxaca and to others from whom I have heard it, in one shape or another, in Tamazulapán and the Sawtooth Mountains and Toronto. In some lesser way the words – and in some greater way also the places – through which it is told in this version belong to me. What interests me, though, isn't the shifting and tenuous ways in which the story belongs to one or another of us, but the deeper ways in which we all (all of us here, now, in this moment which repeats through space and time) belong to the story – and belong to the places through which it is or might be told. It is a simple – some say much too simple – story after all. As well as a true one.

It was either a little or a long time ago,
and the old woman who made the world,
day before yesterday, had only just made it.
The wind picked up, and the sunlight cut
through the air, where it had never been before,
and the old woman who made the world
pitched her camp in a high meadow
not very far from the middle of things,
and looked at the world, and said to her dog,
Well, dog, do you think it'll do?
(She was fishing for compliments, I guess,
which is usually dangerous, but she did it.
She said to the dog, *Do you think it'll do?*)

And the dog said, *Grandmother, yes,*
it's the way I have always imagined the world.
The spruce trees look like spruce trees, the mountain
larches look like mountain larches, the balsam
firs have the unmistakable odor of firs.
But grandmother, these and the others
seem to have places to be in the world.
The rabbit, the mountain cat, the blacktailed
deer, the varied thrush, the squirrel
all have their places, like the mosses
on the rocks and the bright green
lichen hanging in the lodgepole pine.
I'm the only one here, grandmother,
with no one to chase or to run from
or run to, and I'm lonely in this world.

The old woman poked up the fire and sighed
and said, *Dog, I should make you someone to love*
and look after if that's how it is. And she made

men and women, then, as a gift,
to cure the loneliness of the dog.

And the dog said, *Grandmother, thank you,*
and guided his humans out into the world.

The old woman sat there, thinking, alone
in the high meadow, tending her fire,
watching the anemone and yellow lily
sprout through the snow, and the phlox and the grouseberry
flower. Then she thought she saw something travelling
up the valley, dodging the fallen-log
bridges, sloshing through each of the streams.
The dog reappeared at the edge of the meadow
and trotted up close to the old woman's fire.

You're back for a visit already, said
the old woman. *Dog, is anything wrong?*

The dog said, *Grandmother, now that you ask,*
yes: it's those humans you gave me.
They listen, you know, but they don't seem to learn,
and I came back to ask you to give them something
I think they should have. Grandmother, please,
would you teach them to speak? Would you teach them
words, so they can tell one another their lies
instead of keeping them secret?
                                        The old woman
shifted a burned stick farther
into the fire and reached down a little ways into
the ground, and found a jagged, black stone,
like a piece of black basalt, and washed it in the stream,
and set it in the north end of the meadow,
and then she said, *Dog, that stone*
is the stone of speech and storytelling.
Those humans will be able to say what they choose to say

as long as it's there. And no one I know
would want to disturb it.
                              Grandmother, thank you,
said the dog, and he turned and headed down
the valley, to be with his humans again.

The old woman sat in the high meadow
not too far from the middle of things.
She watched the swelling swamp-laurel shells
and the ripening willow galls and the wind.
She watched the purple saxifrage, the yellow
heather and the partridgefoot flower,
and she saw way off, once again, a dark
shape making its way up the valley.
The dog reappeared at the edge of the meadow
and ambled with his long tongue up by the fire.

You're back again, dog. Is anything wrong?

Grandmother, yes. It's the humans again.
You remember I asked you to teach them to talk,
but now they just talk and talk all the time.
It isn't enough, and it's too much.
Grandmother, please, would you teach them to laugh?

The old woman who made the world
picked up a stick and poked at her fire
and reached a little deeper down into the ground
and took a crooked, yellow stone – pale,
like yellow quartz – and scrubbed it in the stream
and set it in the east end of the meadow.
Then she said, *That stone, dog,*
is the stone of laughter and the stone of dreams.
Those humans will be able to laugh
just fine, and maybe have a few
new things to talk about too,
when you see them again.

Thank you, said the dog,
and he went right back to his humans again.

The old woman who made the world
sat watching the mountain windflowers spilling
their plumes, and the willow leaves turning
and the aspen leaves starting to turn,
and then the aspen leaves falling,
and the fir scales floating down out of the firs,
and then she saw something far off, moving
once again. It had four feet and a tail,
and it was headed straight for the meadow.
The dog came wearily up by the fire.

Here you are again, dog, the old woman said.
Is something still wrong?
                    Yes, grandmother.
*I asked you to teach them to talk and to laugh,
and they talk and they laugh just fine, grandmother.
No matter what happens, no matter what
their dreams say, they keep on talking, no matter
what their stories say, they just laugh.*

Grandmother, please, would you teach them to cry?

The old woman looked a long time into the fire,
and she reached down deeply into the ground
and found a smooth, grey pebble,
like a piece of stream gravel, and cleaned it.
She set it in the south end of the meadow,
and then she said, *Dog, that stone
is the stone of weeping and the stone of prayer,
and those humans'll have tears in their eyes
when you see them again.*
                    Thank you, said the dog,
and he vanished into the bush
and made his way back to the humans again.

The old woman who made the world
sat in her camp in the high meadow,
listening to the geese bark in the darkness
overhead and watching the winter wrens
flit through the mountain rhododendron
in the shortening afternoon, and the troops
of waxwings stripping the blueberries bare.
The first snow fell and melted, and the rabbits
moulted, and the marmots disappeared.
And the old woman saw something slogging
up the valley, through the leaf litter
and new snow, breaking trail. The dog reappeared,
chewing his paws, at the edge of the meadow
and came and curled up close by the fire.

You've been gone a bit longer this time, the old woman
said, *but you're back even so. How
are the humans doing?*
                        Better, grandmother,
said the dog, *but something is missing.*

The old woman who made the world
stirred her fire and watched how the coals
glowed pus-yellow, blood-red, bone-white and grey
before they went black. *Choose carefully,
dog,* she said. *Choose very carefully,
dog, because the circle is closing.*

Grandmother, said the dog, *heading
up here today, wading through the deep snow,
I knew what I wanted to ask. Grandmother,
please, would you teach them to dance?*
                                        The old woman
shifted a glowing log deep in the fire
and reached down a great distance into the ground
and grabbed a half-round, blood-red
stone, like jasper or red chert,

and rubbed it with snowmelt and new snow
and set it in the west end of the meadow
and sat back down by the side of the fire
and shifted another log.
                    That stone, dog,
is the stone of dancing and the stone of song.
Those humans can dance now, and sing.
And they can talk and tell stories
and laugh and dream and cry and pray,
and I hope it is enough, because the circle
is closed.
                    And those were your gifts, dog.
They were yours, and you gave them away.
Whatever those humans say from now
on, you'll only hear the pain
and pleasure in their voices. Soon you'll forget
you ever heard the words. Now nothing
but barks and yips and howls will form
in your own throat. Now when they laugh,
you'll make no sound. They'll weep,
and you'll whimper. Now when they dance,
you'll scamper between their legs. You'll jump
up and down, but the music will never
enter your body. The words and the music
and the tears and the laughter will be theirs.
They owe you all this, dog, and I somehow
think they may never remember to thank you.

THE BLUE ROOFS OF JAPAN:

A SCORE FOR INTERPENETRATING VOICES

This is a score for jazz duet, which I hope will function also as a reading text. The full text of the poem is carried on both the righthand and lefthand pages of the book, but since the two voices frequently overlap, the two parts are not always legible on any one page. The lefthand pages give prominence to the male voice, the righthand pages to the female voice. Facing pages should be read not in sequence but together.

If the score is used as a performance text, the male performer should read from the lefthand pages while the female performer reads from the right. By looking through his or her own lines, each may see the other's voice lurking in blue ink underneath. The male voice sets the timing, as it is the more verbose. (This is not a paradigm, but here it is the case.) The female voice cuts lyrically across. Sweetly, I suppose, but deeply enough to draw the necessary blood.

In a house with such a blue
roof, she said with red
hair, you'd wake up cheerful
every morning.
To the talking mirror
of water. To the broken panes
of water laid in the earth like leaded glass.

To the empty cup containing
everything,
to warm it with the tea.

To hold in the hands like a cup of tea,
always full and always empty,
the earthy asymmetry of the world.

To the rich, disordered earth,
to the sound of mountain water,
to the boundless —
truth of the ground.
To the world with its welcome
imperfections.
Violence hides in fastidious order.

To the polished lacquer
platter where the drunken
lion grins.

I

In a house with
such a blue with such a *roof*
roof, *you'd wake up cheerful*
every morning *ke up cheerful*
every morning.
to the talking mirror
To *of water,* ng mirror
of water. *To the talking mirror*
of water, laid in the earth like leaded glass.

To the empty cup conta *to the*
cup containing
to *everything, the hands*

To hold in the hands like a cup of tea,
always empty, always full, ty,
the earthy asymmetry of the world.

To the order of the earth, rth,
to the sound of mountain water,
to the boundless —
not infinite, boundless —
truth of the ground.
To the world with its welcome
imperfections. *Violence hides*
under the lid of fastidious order. r.

To the polished lacquer
platter where the drunken
lion grins.

And to the knowledge it is June; the moon
is choking on its own light; the river
fish are running; at Gifu the leashed
cormorants dive.

To the water that walks over stones
through the long wooden town
like a roshi on wide wooden slippers:

the river marched through the Chinese grid
of the city, not twisting but turning,
as sharp as a section-line road
through the Saskatchewan prairie.

To the Sleeping Dragon
Garden: to the wordless speech of water
broached in the silence of the stone.

To the spoken
shakuhachi, its calligraphy
of sound.

To the trees —
karamatsu, gingko, sugi, bamboo —
who speak for themselves; to the Emperor's
bound and housebroken pines.

To knowing the Emperor's carp and his wood ducks
are pretty, but they are not his,
and his roof is dark brown.

84

The moon is swelling.   *Violence hides.*

to the water that walks
over stones through the long
wooden town,

the river marched through the Chinese grid
of the city,
as sharp as a section-line road
through the prairie:

to the
water   *to the water*
to the stone

to the speaking   *to the trees:*
karamatsu
gingko and *sugi* *bamboo*

karamatsu
are *gingko,* but *sugi* are *bamboo*
But the Emperor's roof
is dark brown.

This music is all about water,
she said. How the hollowed wood
redistributes the air:
ruffled or clear, how the breath
descends: how it pools, and pours

through the holes in the voice,
through the joints in the body, the stem
of bamboo, through the discontinuities
in the skeleton, knots in the plank
at the annual branching, nodes
of nonbeing: not breath but the silences
between breathing: these
are the song; the rest
is mere singing.

II

This music is water, this water
is music: How the hollowed wood
the hollow bamboo
redistributes the water the breath
The air, like the water, descends

through the holes in the voice,
through the joints in the body, the stem
of bamboo, through the discontinuities
In the unbroken muscle of water,
at *the wholeness of bone,* nodes
of nonbei *is the sudden* but *completeness*
betwee *of being,* ing: these
are the song; the rest
is mere sing *the singing*

87

III

Writing is planting.
Writing is born in the lands of wet-farming.
The field prefigures the table and page.
The garden prefigures the table and page.
Writing derives
from the domestication of water.
Rain and the sea
are the mothers of letters.
The mind of the scribe
moves like a long-legged waterbird,
stoops like a rice-farmer, steps like a crane.

When you next see the hunters,
say to the hunters:
O say can you see
how the earth is rewritten
under our hands
until it says nothing?

Say to the hunters: The herders
have taught us the metres, but we
have forgotten. Say to the hunters:
Teach us a song
as subtle as speaking, teach us
a song as lean and as changeable
as the world.

III

Writing is planting.
Writing is born in the lands of wet-farming.
The field prefigures the table and page.
The garden prefigures the table and page.
Is a woman's body
the garden? derives *Writing descends*
from the domestication of water.
Rain and the sea *Rain and the sea,*
are the *rain and the sea* s.
are the mothers of letters. e
moves like a long-legged waterbird,
Rain and the sea are the mothers of letters.

When you next see the hunters,
say to the hunters:
O say *Can you see?*
Can you see how the earth is re-
written? ur hands
until it says nothing?

Say to the hunters: The herders
have taught us *The herders have taught us*
the metres, but we have forgotten.
Say to the hunters:
the mothers of rhythms, rain
and the sea as lean and as changeable
as the world.

IV

But who was it who taught us
the artist's ambitions:
a house in the country, a house
in the town, an apartment in history?

Listen: this music
is all about water. The words
are the earth, and the music
is water.

An artist is anyone
who remembers, it is not you nor me
nor the boss but the gods who are watching.
For these we perform. The others
are eavesdroppers, boob-squeezers, thieves
or voyeurs, or they work here.

The tongues of the gods include
no dates and no names.
This is the logos. is
the logos.

IV

But who was it who taught us
the artist's ambitions:
a house in the country, a house
in the town, an apartment in history?

Listen: this music
*this music too*ter. The words
this music too and the music
is water.

An artist is anyone
who remembers, *anyone who* nor me
anyone who but the gods who are watching.
For these we perform. The others
are eavesdroppers, boob-squeezers, thieves
or voyeurs, or they work here.

The tongues of the gods include
no dates and no names.
This is the THIS *is*
the logos.

V

All afternoon, the slow
celebration of these
two equations:
earth plus water plus fire
gives earth which holds water;
water plus fire plus leaf
gives a bowl full of tea.

A gesture, a form within matter
recentres the air.

neither counting nor naming.

Earthsong and seasong, they say:
the native and foreign.

Naming, not counting.

Water and earth: what ties us together
holds us apart. *What holds us apart*
is what ties us together.
The mountains are younger than birds.
The sea when we lived in the sea
was made of fresh water.
No man is not one of these islands.

What ties us to time and the world
beside us is fire.

Counting, not naming.

v

All afternoon, the slow
This music is water,
two equations:
earth p*this laughter is fire.*
gives earth which holds water;
water plu*Water plus fire*
giv*plus leaf* full of tea.

A gesture, *recentres the air,*tter
recentres the air.

neither counting nor naming.

Earthsong and seasong, they say:
the native and foreign.

Naming, not counting.

Water and earth: what ties us together
holds us apart. *What holds us apart*
is what ties us together.
The mountains are younger than birds.
The sea when we lived in the sea
was made of fresh water.
No man is not one of these islands.

What ties us to time and the world
beside us is fire.

Counting, not naming.

Water is wordless, while the earth
is information. Earth is words.
This too is the logos. A journey on foot
cannot be repeated, just as a story
cannot be recited, only retold.

Naming and counting.

Facing the water, be music.
Be still facing fire. *Be laughter.*
Be laughter. *Three.*
Facing the earth, be darkness. *Five.*
Facing the sky, be quiet, wide and blue.

Water is wordless, while the earth
is information. Earth is words.
This too is the logos. A journey on foot
cannot be repeated, just as a story
cannot be recited, only retold.

Naming and counting.

Facing the water, be music.
Be still facing fire. *Be laughter.*
One. Two. Three.
Facing the *Four*, be darkness. *Five.*
Facing the sky, be quiet, wide and blue.

THINKING & TALKING:

A PROSE CABOOSE

Nyogen Senzaki, a Zen teacher whose path I have often crossed, though he was a man I never met, used to urge his students to breathe through their feet. His admonition has come to me often, walking and climbing the British Columbia Coast Range. And it has come to me climbing the thin stone stairways in the Andes, up from Machu Piqchu, down from Pisaq, knowing what loads others once carried – and still carry sometimes – over those trails. I don't mean the broad Inca highways, but the steep and twisting little cliffedge trails moving through rainforest, cholla and dry scrub. The Runa, who built them and walked them, breathed through their feet. We who were raised in the newer, transplanted cultures of the Americas usually breathe through our bellies and hands.

Senzaki's advice comes back to me also while I am writing. I'd like to write poems which breathe through the feet. Some I have written, some that I tried to make empty and clean as a zendo, have come out as cluttered as a backwoods cabin yard. But it may be the cluttered ones after all which breathe through their feet, or which breathe through the feet of the reader. The clean ones, some of them, scarcely seem to breathe at all.

'All good writing,' Scott Fitzgerald said, 'is swimming under water and holding your breath.' Some spectacular writing is indeed that. But more real poetry, it seems to me, is walking on the ground and breathing.

Either way, walking or swimming, breathing or tensing, poetry also has to do with crossing borders and with bearing precious loads. That is what *metaphor* seems to mean – to carry things across – and that is what the loons and the goldeneyes do as they dive and rise, feeding in the bay that is ten yards down and five yards out from my open door.

It seems to me, though, that my personal history has, and ought to have, rather little to do with my writing. Many of my contemporaries prefer to let the events of their lives set the shapes of their poems. But myth, as opposed to 'mere literature,' never works in this

way. In myth, form and content are not identical, nor is one an ex-
tension of the other, though there is living tension between them,
just as there is in our bodies and in the annual migrations of those
birds. (By the form of a myth or a poem, I mean more than its
acoustic or typographic form; I mean its narrative or meditative
shape, plot, structure, the higher grammar of image and event. And
by content I mean, among other things, what José Ortega y
Gasset had the wisdom to call the higher algebra of metaphor.)

Where I have been, what I have done, gives me the lumber for
the poems, but the lumber does not generate the shape. The shape is
given to me from elsewhere – unearthed or inherited – or inhaled.
And this is the way in which I transpose my own life into the myths
and the myths into my own life. Seen in this way, it turns out not to
be 'my life' at all, but merely my sense of the world I live in, with the
emphasis on the world, not on the I who is doing the sensing.

So for example my own experiences in the Sinai in the wake of
the Six Day War, and in the red rock deserts of southern Utah, are
fed to the ghost of Moses in a poem called 'Deuteronomy'; a story
from the Cowichan River on Vancouver Island is fueled, in
Tzuhalem's Mountain, with my own experience of the Coast Range;
and in a piece called 'The Stonecutter's Horses,' Francesco Petrarca is
made to sound as though he had just been hiking the Siskiyous,
which straddle the Oregon/California line.

For years I kept tacked to my studio wall a *Punch* cartoon which
I'd captioned 'Portrait of the Artist.' In the thin, square lens through
which cartoonists view the world, a man, nearly drowned, was being
lugged up the beach by a taciturn lifeguard. 'My whole life passed be-
fore me,' coughed the limp, drenched figure. 'My whole life passed
before me, and I wasn't in it.' If I understand correctly, this vision oc-
curred not while the drowning man was holding his breath, but
while, in spite of himself, he was breathing.

*   *   *

I was born in the post-Depression diaspora at the close of the Second
World War, the only child of itinerant parents – ambitious father,
obedient mother – and raised in the mountains of western North

America, moving often and liking it well. I remember especially the Absaroka Ranges in Montana, the Valley of the Little Bighorn and the Wind River Mountains and the Southern Absarokas in Wyoming, the Maligne Mountains and the Goat Range in Alberta, and the Virgin River country – my Mormon great-grandfather's mountains – in southern Utah. In later years, I've felt myself at home in a thousand named and nameless places in that long spine of mountains, steppe and desert which I've walked, in bits and pieces, most of the way from the Yukon to Peru. Much as I've loved the few cities I've lived in – Boston, Beirut, London, Vancouver – I've never been at ease for long in urban spaces. Premonitions of doom come over me readily in the large, self-confident capitals of eastern North America, where so many decisions that touch the world I prefer to live in are now made.

The place I was born used to be the country of the Kumivit – people who spoke a language related to Hopi, Shoshone and Nahuatl, who lived in large domed houses of bulrush and watergrass, drank a broth of the sacred datura in quest of their visions, and shared a profound tradition of abstract art with their physically close but linguistically distant neighbours, the Chumash.

A Portuguese sailed into one of their bays in 1542 and gave it a name on his chart but left it alone. The Spanish stole it from the Kumivit in 1769, and renamed my particular part of it El Pueblo de Nuestra Señora la Reina de los Angeles de Porciúncula – in honor, improbably enough, of the madonna of St Francis of Assisi. The U.S. Army stole it from the Spanish in 1846, and I arrived myself, somewhat more quietly, exactly a century later. The Kumivit were then extinct, and the Spanish colonial culture, bloody as it was, had been prettified into picturesque decor. The Kumivit village of Yangna had become the chrome-and-neon compost known to all aficionados of American nonculture as L.A.

I've often pretended I was born elsewhere, in some deeper layer of that midden, or on some peak or beach or raft where less imperial detritus had accrued. But my birth certificate says it was there.

And it was, in fact, a compost. Lifeforms thrived within the garbage, and almost anything could be found there. To take one improbable example, a Siberian-born renegade Zen monk, trained at

Engakuji, who read Thomas Carlyle (and everything else) in his spare time, was wandering the city. He was the teacher I've already mentioned, Nyogen Senzaki, and he was a great crosser of borders. In 1946 he was freshly returned, with many other Japanese, from the Heart Mountain prison camp in northern Wyoming – a place I was taken myself, years later, knowing nothing yet of Senzaki, by my father, who thought there was something there I should learn. The barbed wire was still up then too, though only the ghosts were still imprisoned. Heart Mountain was the first *ruin* I had ever seen, and it sits vivid in my mind, alongside Baalbek, Chaco Canyon, Delphi and other places, larger but seen later, which dwarf it in space and time.

The north end of Watts, where my parents were living in the mid 1940s; the Heart Mountain compound; Red Lodge, Montana; Calgary; Butte; the wild valleys I hiked as a child – those of the San Juan River and the Green, which are now under water, while the huge reservoirs they contain are filling with speedboats and marinas. . . . A litany of places, to conjure the long spaces between them. The earth itself is a living body, and a kind of brain. It is living information, like the cortex and the genes. We flood it with water and asphalt and concrete and standardized grass, and with signs that say Fried Chicken or Mountain Estates or Colour TV in Every Room or Jesus Saves, and we think *that* is information. I was born in the home of the celluloid vision and the armor-plated American dream, but I cannot remember a time when I was not horrified by that face of America: by its superficial brilliance, its arrogant self-assurance, its love of itself, its insentience, its greed.

So while most of my colleagues in the Canadian and American poetry racket devote themselves to speaking for and within the colonial culture to which they belong – and which, of course, contains a great deal of profundity and of beauty – I have spent my own life learning to speak across and against it. I have tried to pack up into my poems all it contained that looked worth stealing, and to resituate that wealth, that salvageable wisdom, in someplace spiritually distinct: some other dimension of the physical space I inhabit, and which the maze of governments, real-estate agencies and development corporations supposes it owns.

This is a hopeless task, of course. The treasure is far more than I can carry, and the machinery of progress and industrial development is destroying the nonhuman world far faster than a few ecologists, poets or terrorists can protect it. But there is nothing else to do, for there is nowhere else to go. Home is where the stones have not stopped breathing and the light is still alive.

Those of us raised in colonial North America have been taught not an ecology of living facts, but a vision of endless progress, endless development, endless gain – and a vision also of social justice and personal liberty. These visions have been linked in the presumption that the world of endless development is a universal world, one that has room within it for everything. But a world with room for nothing *outside* itself, room for nothing beyond its control, is a world in which liberty and prosperity are hollow, and one in which justice is severed from both its origins and its ends.

I and the audience I try to write for live not in but on the edges of that world, in order always to remember that it does have an outside. As a creature of the edges instead of the collapsing centre, I have made it my business not to parody or portray the central insanities of that world – which is what much current writing is about – nor even to praise the still functioning graces – which are many after all, and which again much current writing is about. I have made it my business simply to find what I thought I could salvage and preserve, and to pack it out into another, coterminous world. There, with no hope of enduring success – and with no need of a new physical structure, so numerous are the ruins – I have been trying to live on closer, less arrogant terms with the real – which is, I repeat, for the most part nonhuman.

I feel fortunate that I was raised a political orphan, moving often across international borders, especially the U.S./Canada border, never learning to be at home with the sense of nationhood on either side. The only political act that made sense to me as a child was to refuse to sing anyone's national anthem or mutter pieties to anyone's national flag. This unnationalism was, of course, the implicit tradition in North America until the eighteenth century, and it has survived, albeit perilously, into present times. It is the tradition of Dumont instead of Riel, Thoreau instead of Emerson, Melville instead of Whitman, Big Bear instead of Sir John Alexander Macdonald.

But because I was schooled, in the early years, much as everyone else was in colonial North America, I grew up with one foot in the confident world of western historicism. It took me a long time to find the other foot – the one I'd been standing on, as it turned out, all the while. I was thirty years old before I began the serious study of the languages and cultures native to the hemisphere I called home. Others, my elders – like Gary Snyder, Jarold Ramsay, Jerry Rothenberg, and even that strange old spectre Witter Bynner – had contemplated or taken this road before me. If I'd been less unsociable, or just been quicker to learn, they might have saved me a great deal of time. As it is, I'm still very glad of my little Greek and less Chinese – but the ten years I spent learning Arabic would, I now know, have been far better spent learning Hopi and Navajo.

I do still read the European and even colonial North American poets – primarily those at the two extremes of the history, ancient and modern. But I spend more time reading the works of biologists and anthropologists. I think of them often as the real poets of my age. And I read the remains of the native American oral literature. That, if anything, seems to me the real core of my heritage now. In the summer of 1984, I found in a Philadelphia library unpublished transcripts, in Haida, of performances by the great Haida mythteller Walter McGregor of the Qaiahllanas, recorded in 1901 in the Queen Charlotte Islands. And I felt then an excitement such as I think Gian Francesco Poggio Bracciolini felt in 1417, when, poking through manuscripts at a monastery in Italy, he uncovered the lost text of Lucretius' *De rerum natura*.

As recently as 1980, I taught, at a major Canadian university, a course in literature in which only the European and colonial tradition was mentioned, with the odd passing reference to India and China. I can no more imagine doing that now than I can imagine trying to restitute the British Empire – but it has been a long, slow road to learn.

*   *   *

Another teacher I never met, and who knew a lot about breathing, was Ezra Pound. But Pound also exemplifies the extraordinary factiousness, the imbalance, the self-righteousness and paranoia, and the fearful patriotism and pride of Euramerican civilization. When I was younger, I carried his books with me everywhere, and in 1965, on my way to Beirut, I went to Italy to see him. But as I neared the house I realized I had nothing whatever to tell him and nothing very interesting to ask him either, so I walked on. The thought that he might have something to tell *me* seems not to have entered my mind. In those days, I believed that a man could put everything and then some into his books, and that another man could come along later and dig it all out again.

Oddly enough, I was not much troubled then by Pound's readiness to hate the Taoists, the Buddhists, the Jews and any number of other groups. In him as in other large-hearted bigots, these hatreds were contradicted at every turn by individual friendships, but I was a long time in coming to wonder why, in that case, those hatreds were still there. At the time, I thought of them simply as a disease which Pound suffered and I didn't. It seems more obvious to me now that Pound suffered them in part because his cultural inheritance encouraged him to do so. It has given me plenty of unwanted encouragement of the same kind.

Pound himself touched another American bent in me too, and that was my prolonged fascination with craftsmanship and technique, with inward mechanics and outward physical forms. With Pound's example before me, I spent years on the study of metrics. I don't mean I did daily exercises with the Welsh or French or Arabic verse forms; I was never much interested in envelopes. But I studied prosodic systems and speech sounds, the acoustic as well as syntactic shaping of language. I focussed for years on the audible half of the craft of polyphony – which in my trade generally means making a music one of whose voices sounds audibly in the throat while the others sound silently, and differently, yet relatedly, in the mind.

After twenty years of working at it, I can now sometimes think about orchestrating a poem instead of shaping a single line – which is why, I suppose, the word *form* no longer seems to me, as it once did, merely a synonym for versification. Along the way, it seems to me I have come to learn relatively less from other poets and more from artists of other kinds. I've learned more about composition from the late sonatas of Beethoven, more about silence from the late paintings of Borduas, and – though I cannot write like he could play – more about tonality and broken timbre from John Coltrane than from any poet I could name.

And I don't regret the time I've spent studying prosody, though it's clear to me now it has little to do with the essence of poetry. Like its visual counterpart, typography (another physical and mechanical business which, for me, has held mysterious fascinations), prosody is in its simplest forms a ceremonial tool and in its complex forms a sometimes burdensome luxury. At its best, it is a device for retaining and touching the poetry. It may be as useful and beautiful as a bowl, but a bowl is not water, and the untranslatable stuff of prosody is rarely, I think, *essential* to the poetry itself. Yet I value it highly, as I always have. To borrow a sentence from Pound, I value technique as a test of an author's sincerity. I value it as evidence of his commitment to something more than a private audience with the gods.

None of this means, of course, that poetry doesn't sing. It does sing, or seeks to sing – and will try to do so visually, as the hills do in winter, if it is prevented from doing so audibly, as the thrushes do in spring. It may for all that be no more scannable than the Kaskawulsh Glacier and no more tuneful than an Arctic tern.

A language is a sort of lifeform, like a discontinuous animal or a symbiotic plant. Dead, it is like the intricate test of a sea urchin or the lifeless shell of a crab. Alive, it is a working form of intelligence, a part of the intellectual gene pool which has taken on specified, localized form. It is not, as many of my colleagues in the literature business like to say, the mother of poetry. Poetry has nothing essential to do with language. Language just happens to be the traditional means – but hardly the only available means – by which poetry is touched, in which it is temporarily captured, and through which it is served (or, as we all know, sometimes disserved). The poetry seems somehow always willing to revisit certain old poems (it helps if we remember how to pronounce them), just as the gods seem reluctant to abandon certain old temples (it helps if we remember how to approach them). Yet there are many, more modern structures which neither poetry nor the gods seem willing to touch, no matter how skilfully those structures may be engineered.

What does this mean in the face of a passage by one of the

masters of prosody – Pound, for example, or Cavalcanti, Shake-speare or Gautier? What does it mean in the face of a poem in which, as Pound liked to say, the beauty is melted into the phrase? Take these lines for instance, from Basil Bunting's *The Spoils:*

> *Have you seen a falcon stoop*
> *accurate, unforeseen*
> *and absolute, between*
> *wind-ripples over harvest? Dread*
> *of what's to be, is and has been –*
> *were we not better dead?*
>
> *His wings churn air*
> *to flight.*
> *Feathers alight*
> *with sun, he rises where*
> *dazzle rebuts our stare,*
> *wonder our fright.*

Is the sound not integral to the vision? Is the vision not heard as well as seen? It is, and it lies *outside the language* in which a response to it has been made. It exists beyond the words which, in their sharp loveliness, house it and trace it and lead us, like lovers, to follow its contours time and again with our tongues.

But if poetry has nothing quintessential to do with language, what does it have to do with? It has to do, for one thing, with the other forms of attention. When I say that colonial American culture seems to me insentient, this is what I have in mind. For all the scientists, poets, scholars and trained observers of all kinds, all the professional attention-payers we have in western society, attention is precisely what seems to be absent from our daily lives. 'Breathe through your feet' is a gentler, more informative, less self-centred and less frustrated form of the well-known adjuration, 'Pay atten-tion.' It doesn't mean pay attention to *me*; it just means pay atten-tion.

It is, for instance, what snails do under duress. The snail, who is almost all foot to begin with, though he almost always has gills or a lung, can breathe through every pore in his body. I can imagine Nyogen Senzaki, in his snail incarnation, pushing still further, saying in Snail, 'Breathe through your shells.' He was, as I've said, a great crosser of borders, and had little patience with excess baggage.

In the year of Senzaki's release from the Heart Mountain prison camp, Ezra Pound was interred at another such camp near Pisa. He was then indicted for treason as a result of his radio broadcasts from Italy during the war. But let us remember that the society which indicted him did so not for his lunatic promotion of racial hatred. His crime, as far as the U.S. government was concerned, was simply that he had urged rapprochement with Mussolini and an immediate end to the war. Let us also remember that the society which bore, bred and indicted him was the same one which had imprisoned Nyogen Senzaki and thousands of others merely for being (or looking) Japanese. It was a society in which apartheid was legally sanctioned and almost universally practised against Amerindians, Asians and Africans. It has become since then a society whose two principal businesses are the manufacture and deployment of the instruments of mass anesthesia and mass destruction. And it is a society whose relentless persecution of native Americans seems destined to continue until every Indian left alive has finally consented to the state religion, which is to say the industrial-mercantile economy, and with it the real-estate ethic, that land can be freely bought and sold.

It is a monster more benign than many others; of this there is no doubt, but it is a monster nonetheless. I hope that my own slow and unobtrusive treason against the nation-state I was born in, while it will never be as notorious as Pound's, will prove in the long run less boneheaded and more fruitful. I would like that as much as I'd like to write poetry which the rasp-tongued, mad old master might have admired.

*   *   *

I've brooded here on the distinction between the colonial and native American cultures. But in the tangled roots of the European tradition lay cultures which must, in significant ways, have resembled the ones that, for three hundred years, we have worked to extinguish throughout North America. The remains of those old, now voiceless, cultures of Europe – from the paintings of Lascaux to the fragments of Empedokles and Herakleitos – though they come to us in pieces, speak of a wholeness which, in our rapacious industrial society, is almost unknown.

I have lived and worked with the discontinuous ghosts of the old philosopher-poets of Greece for a long time, and I admire about those poets in particular their refusal to be compartmentalized. I admire their assumption that poetry, philosophy, physics, biology, ethics and even theology are all one pursuit. I admire, in other words, their moral and spiritual and intellectual integrity. And I admire, by the way, the fact that they were good ecologists, good environmentalists, though they'd have made no sense of that compartment either.

I find that same integrity in many of the philosopher-poets of the Orient – in Lao Tzu, Chuang Tzu, Saraha, Sengcàn, and in those remarkable Sung dynasty writers, Danxiá and Xuědoù (Redcloud and Snowcave). I think I sense it also in St Francis of Assisi, though hardly in the works of those who sailed to the New World in his name. But to me it seems clearest of all in some of the quiet, cornered voices of the native American tradition. It is there to be read in the salvaged scraps of oral literature, and it is still there to be heard in the mouths of a steadily shrinking number of native gardeners, hunters and herders who live in the steadily shrinking real world – the lean tracts not yet consumed by an insatiable white society with the stupidest goals in the world: money and jobs. Not piety, grace, understanding, wisdom, intelligence, truth, beauty, virtue, compassion. None of these. Not real wealth either, but only factitious wealth; and not a relationship with nor a place in the nonhuman order, but life in a wholly consumptive, introverted scheme: money and jobs.

I find sustenance now for that archaic sense of integrity more among naturalists than among poets, more in broken country than in social order, more with marmots and great blue herons than with human beings. I hope that my own poems, like those of the Presocratics – and like the tales of Walter McGregor of the Qaiahllanas, and the great poem of Lucretius – are not about human beings exclusively, but about the world, and about the painful business of loving and living with the world. Breathing through the feet, while the colonial culture keeps tearing the air with its hands.

But speech is in its origins a set of social gestures, and a man who turns his back upon his fellows severs himself from the wellsprings of language. Silences puncture his speech. He grows inarticulate. What kind of sentence is that upon a poet? Perhaps the best kind. A man who turns his back upon his fellows severs himself from the wellsprings of eloquence, but not from the sources of meaning.

So like the drunk who befriends the dog, because everyone else is too far off the floor to talk to, I keep the company, for preference, of the rocks and trees, the loons and the seaducks who at this moment are close out the door. I ignore you, reader, for something larger than you, which includes you or not, as you choose — though of course, in another sense, whatever you choose, it includes you. And you include it, and our fate rests not just on our own feet but in one another's hands.

This is the partial record of an interview conducted by mail during January, February and March 1986. The questions were posed by Andrew Campbell from Barboursville, West Virginia, and the responses generally mailed from Vancouver.

You have, in your poetry in the past, incorporated botany, mathematics, mythologies, religions, and much else. Why? Do you have a strategy behind such inclusions?

Can we substitute 'theology' for 'religions'? Knowledge of the gods is one thing; adherence to creed is another.

No, I don't have a strategy, only a rationalization. The arts and the sciences are in their origin one pursuit. Biology, physics, mathematics, the painting of paintings, the telling of myths, metaphysical reasoning – all of these are ways of listening to and speaking with the world. They are aspects of intelligence. What else is poetry for?

Music that is too human is useless. That which is too exclusively human is not human *enough*. Our deepest passions push us way outside ourselves. They lead us to talk about mountains and stars and to know our deep kinship with birds and shellfish and flowers. Geology and astronomy and biology are, or can be, ways of attending that wholeness and *allowing* it to be whole instead of turning it into a deadly totality. Knowing the wholeness of the world is not the same, after all, as building a great dictatorship of self-consistent theory – something science and religion both seem to become if we let them.

Science, like art, is founded on wonder. Light is the precondition of vision – and what is light but the radiance of what is? Poetry and the sciences are linked inextricably right there. And they are linked there also with what calcifies into religion.

Art is not a house. Art is an opening made in the air. It is seeing and saying and being what is in the world. Homer's naming of the gods is a discovery, not an invention, and it is an achievement of perception on a par with Dmitri Mendeléyev's mapping of the periodic table — that chart of the elements which hangs now in chemistry labs all over the world. The abject assent we are taught to give to the findings of science is woeful — but the teaching that poetry is just personal expression is every bit as woeful. The fruitful territory is between these extremes, where art and science are linked and where they began. Homer and Mendeléyev both knew themselves to be parts of a collaborative venture, building on the findings of their predecessors, drawing from their colleagues, and making something which they and their successors would revise.

The Lithuanian philosopher Emmanuel Levinas spent some of the Second World War in a prison camp, where he wrote a little book called *De l'existence à l'existant.* He makes some interesting remarks there on the arts. 'Painting,' he says, 'is a struggle with sight.' Many poets nowadays hold the lazy, ethnocentric view that literature is merely a struggle with *speaking.* But follow the analogy of Levinas's statement and you will come to a very different proposition: that literature is a struggle with *hearing,* with *listening.* The writer needs a stethoscopic ear, and he can — I prefer that he should — lay it against the stones and wild grasses as well as against his own chest. And the chests, of course, of other human beings.

You occasionally teach poetry workshops. What do you concentrate on? Do you recommend translating to your students?

I like to recommend translating to students, because for me it was a useful way to practise. But I don't teach very often, and I haven't had many students who were equipped to do translation. I've had still fewer who were motivated that way. And I haven't taught a long-term or term-long writing course for ten years. It's hard to provoke people into serious translations during a four-day seminar.

In the past year, I've done a couple of workshops with Cree and Ojibwa writers and translators in northern Ontario, where the opportunities are somewhat different. On some fronts there is less, but on other fronts more, blinkered devotion to colonial tradition. The missionary activity has been very heavy, of course, and the centrally controlled school system and TV and consumer advertising, which pretend to be just as benign as the church, are just as totalitarian. Even the secular literature native peoples have been offered can aggravate the problem. Euramerican literature is peculiar, by and large, in its fixation on domestic and military life. Primitive literature doesn't anatomize the emotions as farm-and-city literature does, nor explore diversionary puzzles and thrills as suburban literature does; it's concerned with a larger, less egoistic sphere.

A major function of literature in the colonized world – which, nowadays, is the whole world – is to keep us from being trapped in our own collapsing history. For the Cree and Ojibwa, whose native languages are still relatively strong, translation is an obvious way to do this, and some of them are interested in it. There's also a vital world of village-theatre there, much closer to Aristophanes than to Shaw, which promises to serve them well. Sometimes I've given them Aristotelian exercises to do: *ethos, mythos, dianoia,* for instance. I don't trouble them with the Greek names, but I take some pleasure in knowing that the pedagogy, such as it is, comes straight from a man who concocted it sitting on a stone bench watching the plays of Sophocles. (And, alas, misunderstanding the plays of Euripides.)

I haven't persuaded any of them to *write* in Cree or Ojibwa, though, so I must be a failure as a teacher. I've told them the hair-raising story of José María Arguedas, the Peruvian novelist who was talked out of writing in Runasimi, his native tongue, and who ended up, in a manner of speaking, with it writing him. They listened very carefully, but they didn't budge. They've made the decision our culture has urged them to make: that their languages lose and ours wins.

Some of your poetry is an improvisation upon the works of other poets and philosophers. Why?

Reworking the gifts and givens of other thinkers feels to me like an essential part of the task. That is a use of poetry: to sing thought back into being, to personify it, state it, locate it, to clear the haze.

My reworkings of other poets are fewer and slighter. Years ago, I did quite a bit of translating, but I've thrown most of it away. In those far days I had never heard of Rudolf Pannwitz, but I worked along the lines that Pannwitz had proposed. That is, if I found myself translating from Arabic, I tried, as a rule, not to make it seem that the original had been written in English, but to make the English function like Arabic: to enlarge the language, to open it up to that very un-English, un-North-American mind. I couldn't have said this then, I suppose, but I knew that my language was the language of refugees. That it was defined less by those for whom it was native than by those who were immigrants to it, those for whom it was a third or second tongue. I understood that it had to make room for them: not to grind or melt them down to fit what it could offer, but to stretch and change, to absorb what they could bring. To become many Englishes, not one.

In the old days on the British Columbia coast, through the welter and jabble of languages, stories were passed along by polylingual travellers. Stories passed through the lenses and prisms of language and landscape, recombining and mutating. Now we have the great fungus of English which has spread across the globe, soaking up everybody's stories like a sponge. Translation has become an industry. Telling stories – through film and TV and mass-market books – has become an industry as well. But the *intelligence* of the stories is subverted in this way, and the intelligence of the language lapses too – as the intelligence of food itself and of eating is subverted by industrial processing and packaging. I find the old handing back and forth of stories a more enviable model for translation than I do the modern practice of diplomacy and intelligence-gathering, which is on one level what 'comparative literature' or 'international literature' has become.

And I see no virtue in being *original* in the cant sense of the word, but only in the obvious sense: I want the work to be authentic; I want it deeply in touch with origins. I don't want to speak for the present moment, to speak 'for my time,' as they say. Time in that sense is a jail we have to break out of. And our time has too many spokesmen already, who see it as paper-thin, who forget that its depth is the past.

You mention the influence of Beethoven's sonatas and Coltrane's im-

provisations on your work. In what ways do these influences enter the shaping and drafting of your poems?

There's a great deal for a poet to learn about prosody from sources outside the language – from poets in other languages, and from sources outside language altogether. From the whinnying of grebes, the singing of Arctic loons, or the horn playing, for instance, of John Coltrane. I wish someone with a good ear and a clear head would write a study of tempi and stretched quantity, and the counterpoint of quantity and accent, in the prosodies of the later William Butler Yeats and the earlier Miles Davis.

There's more to it than prosody, of course, but these are difficult issues to speak of. The larger question is, what kinds of correspondences exist between geological, biological and artistic structures? It's difficult enough to address the much smaller question: what kinds of correspondences really exist between musical and verbal structures, musical and verbal materials and themes? The arts have diverged into fields in which we've written different rules.

My narrative poems may not owe much to musical models anyway, but the longer nonnarrative pieces certainly do. I feel at home among the architectures of Beethoven and Coltrane, John Dowland and John Lewis, Alban Berg and Maki Ishii, in a way that I don't feel at home among the structures of Pope or Dryden, Milton or Corneille. Maybe my literary ideas are simply so granular, so pulverized, that they've become analogous to eighth notes.

Many people take for granted the primacy of narrative, and of course they may be right – they may be logically right or historically right or both. But I can entertain the opposite possibility as well. In a poem like *Tzuhalem's Mountain*, which is written pretty much in sonata form, the structural unit, the molecule, is the image. The structural unit in a poem like *Tending the Fire* may be the event. But maybe event is merely image potted in time, image stretched over time, enacted, personified. I don't have to know which is the chicken, which the egg. Many of the poems I'm permitted to write come to me wanting nonnarrative forms, and I work to provide them. Musicians have been composing nonnarrative forms for a good long time, and the legacy there is richer than the legacy of nonnarrative literary forms. The example set by those musicians gives me courage, and they teach me some of the structural lessons I need to learn.

This is nothing new, after all. Joyce, Pound, Eliot, Gertrude Stein, Hermann Broch all learned structural lessons from composers. Eliot published poems he called quartets; Pound and Joyce both spoke of writing fugues. This terminology is imprecise, I suppose, but I think there's a good reason why Pound and Joyce chose a Baroque term, fugue, to describe what they were doing. They'd broken the mold of narrative, linear, continuous, picturesque writing – which is like homophony and melody in music – and entered the world of eidetic, agglutinative, discontinuous, chordal writing – which is like harmony and polyphony in music. This is taken to be a modern development, but it draws from the deep roots of poetry. It goes back to the shamans, back to the oldest whistles and horns and percussion. The *vision song*, surely, is as old, and as important, as the *story*. The rediscovery of this tradition in modernist writing is tied up with imagism, in the same way that the rediscovery of the power of primitive sculpture is tied up with cubism – but we mustn't let the historical taxonomy hide from us the prehistoric potency which underlies these movements. We mustn't confuse the durable tradition with the modernist fad.

We shouldn't let my little distinction between narrative and agglutinative hide things from us either. Artists like Walter McGregor and John Sky – two Haida mythtellers from the end of the nineteenth century – walk right through it.

Can you see yourself attempting a long poem?

Long-poem disease hits many poets at forty. I'm 39; I expect to contract it any day.

I don't live in a world in which the short poem is a welcome or sensible object. What can I do with one if I write it except send it to the editor of some morose or flippant little magazine – or worse, sell it for money to the editor of some hopped-up monthly, where it will function as an ornament between two columns of racy prose and a four-color ad for Scotch whisky? The short poem is a welcome grace in an ordered life. We do not lead ordered lives. We live in a catastrophic world – a world which the short poem can't convincingly address. A world, therefore, in which, if someone does read a poem, he is likely to read it too earnestly and all wrong, or too quickly, too lightly, and equally wrong. The temptation in such a world is to create an island of answering: to reinvent everything, to write another obese, eccentric monument, in spite of one's best intentions. Yes, I well may.

Can you imagine giving up poetry? Or, at least, giving up publishing your poetry?

For all my complaints against the stupidity of our culture, I enjoy my own life just fine, thank you, so I don't sit around dreaming about changing my personal circumstances. But yes, I can imagine not writing poetry. Of course I can imagine not writing poetry. At this very moment I *am* not writing poetry. It has, for the moment, given me up, or I've given it up. We may never meet again. I would think it a mistake ever to count on writing another line. On the other hand, poetry seems to me to be a name for something in the very texture of being, so I don't see that any of us can genuinely escape it, though many of us these days do relentlessly try.

I can certainly imagine giving up the paraphernalia of books and magazines. Much as I love books, I can readily see giving them up. And the magazine is an institution I've never understood very well in any case.

Readings, performances, have been more important to me. A world in which I never recited poetry, at least to friends or to the hills, would seem to me forlorn. And I'd be bitterly impoverished if I never heard it. But I hear it all the time, not just from human sources. I mean it when I say poetry is in the very texture of being. I hear it from the rocks and trees and the sea I live with and the widgeons who are here all winter every year. But not to hear a human voice as well, speaking the poetry of humans. . . . Well, it's all one world, you know, but I've named some of the things I seem to cling to. The Buddhist convention is to say that enlightened beings have left the world and returned, out of generosity, to teach, or out of unwholeness, because the rest of us are still here. But it's a beautiful place, isn't it? It's as easy to believe that the bodhisattvas come here to feed, precisely because they've been unblinded. I would like to be able to say: I imagine everything and nothing.

In a recent reading, you began with Deuteronomy *and concluded with* Tzuhalem's Mountain, *moving from desert to mountain. Do you attempt to structure all your readings?*

A reading is a concert, a performance, and it should be planned like any other concert, or like any mountaineering expedition. The plan should fit on the back of an envelope, and it should be open to instant revision, but it should be there. And the preparations should be there, in the form of a focussed space and time.

The readings I like best aren't readings at all. There is no book, and the voice carries it all. As you know, there has been a lot of hopeless resistance, especially in university faculties, to treating poetry in this way. In the U.S.A., Yvor Winters said it was wrong, and in Canada John Glassco said it was wrong, and many people seem to agree with them. Then too, the organizers of readings on university campuses are often baffled by a request for a glass of water, much less a room free of fluorescent lights, hard chairs, antiseptic acoustics, hourly bells and the other impedimenta of academic life. Poetry is the poor man's art; it doesn't thrive in a world of distractions. But the voice, the performance itself, is no distraction from the poem, any more than a good violin is a distraction from the sonata. Art is not a house, but art is not an idea either. It has to *occur*.

Would you discuss your interest in Zen? Is it becoming more important in your work?

I don't have much to say about that, I'm afraid. I encountered Daisetz Teitaro Suzuki, through some of his books, when I was 14 or so. That tradition has fed my intelligence ever since. But if I'm a Buddhist, I'm a carnivorous Buddhist. It isn't, for me, what is usually meant by religion. I've taken no vows. The very idea that one could take them, in a ceremonial and human context, rather confounds me.

In a recent essay you discuss Nyogen Senzaki. In The Beauty of the
Weapons *you cite a Rinzai master. In your essay on Dennis Lee, you
link his poems to the meditations of Heidegger, Saraha and Seng-
zhaò. Does Zen contain a structure of thought or a way of living in
the world that has been ignored or forgotten by the West, a way
similar to that of Herakleitos and Pythagoras and other sages impor-
tant to you?*

Zen doesn't *contain* anything. That's one of the reasons we need it,
we who keep wanting to surround and corner everything.

The Presocratics speak from the beginning of literacy in Europe,
and historians of culture like to describe them as something new. To
me they also seem to speak from something old. Prehistory clings to
their voices. So does it to the voices of the last preliterate, tradition-
ally schooled native Americans, recorded through the intercession of
the anthropologists — Franz Boas and many others — while the cul-
tures they spoke from were being destroyed. I hear a similarly atten-
tive, unmanipulative tone in the voices of some Asian thinkers. The
Bengali philosopher-poet Saraha is one example.

I don't say that all these preindustrial thinkers think the same. I
say that they have in common a sanity which is missing from the
prophets and apologists of imperialistic cultures — east and west,
Marxist and capitalist, feudal and mercantile, theist and atheist.
Hegel and Han Fei Tzu, Adam Smith and Marx, Chogyam Trungpa
and John Rawls all make me equally nervous.

I don't claim that preindustrial cultures were always sane and
jolly places to live, nor that the answer for us is always to ape their
ways. But many of the individual mythtellers and singers and philos-
ophers — the artists and scientists, which is what they were — who've
been important to me *do* speak from those cultures. These thinkers —
Haida and Navajo, Ojibwa and Cree, Aboriginal Australian, Chinese
Buddhist and pagan Greek — form an intellectual Third World from
which I've learned, and from which I continue to learn, a great deal. I
feel at home — enlivened and rested at once — in their presence, in a
way I don't feel at home among the real-estate agents and entre-
preneurs and John Stuart Mill and the demagogues and policemen.

Levinas and Heidegger and George Grant and other western

thinkers of the last few generations have rekindled this preindustrial, anti-imperial tradition, which is as long and rich in the west as it is in the east, though for centuries it has lain deep underground. But it doesn't seem enough to me to speak of these things in the Euramerican tradition. Imperialism is age-old and worldwide. So is demagoguery. In every nation on the planet, the world is being sterilized by greed. But the alternatives are also worldwide. They are plural, and we need to know that.

The paleolithic world was whole; it was one world without ever being an empire. People walked across continents and sailed across seas, carrying visions, carrying stories. The voices of that wholeness and multiplicity well up in the damnedest places – in the middle of the Tang Empire, in the middle of the Third Reich and in the midst of the nuclear arms race; in the Sorbonne as well as the jungles of Brazil and the Arnhem Land escarpments. Those voices are also necessarily multilingual, and if we're going to hear them, we have to hear them that way.

E pluribus unum, it says on your coins: one from many; and that is the rule of empire. The rule of the longer term is many from many, *e pluribus plus*. It's a gift we are constantly given. The tower of Babel is always falling. In a Vietnamese restaurant in Vancouver, not long ago, I saw a small handlettered sign. It said, 'Vietnamese New Year Celebration, to be held in the Polish Friendship Centre.' We laugh. Then we remember some of the pain and dislocation behind that sign, and we stop laughing. But the people who put up the sign, and those who established that little centre, have survived. They're here, like the rest of us, refugees, bringing meaning into the language, bringing their *languages* into the language, bringing their parodies of our popular music, which was parody in the first place, bringing their food. In this sorrowful but delectable cultural rubble there are things to do, as for instance, to cook and eat and think and sing. And one of the things to think about is that the March of Western History has become a terrible myth, or antimyth. It has ceased to mean. It swallows the earth and it closes the mind like a steel helmet. It is, as you were saying, a *structure* of thought, which makes it impossible to think outside that structure.

We're not going to get away from structures. But we could do with some lithe, open, agile, portable structures, some articulating structures. We could do with some kayaks and tents in place of the steamships and apartment blocks of belief which we have substituted for thinking. Senzaki and Línjì and Saraha, Herakleitos and Pythagoras are our old people who know about that lighter way of living and moving. Our going back to them is like the American Indians' journey back to their own old people and back to their land. But we can't all go the same place. We have to go, as Hán Shan says, together in different directions.

Chinese names in this list are generally spelled according to the
Pinyin system. Alternate romanizations, which follow the old Wade-
Giles system, are given in parentheses.

BAÏZHÀNG HUAÍHAÏ (Pai-chang Huai-hai, 720–814) Reputedly
the author of the first set of Zen monastic rules, including the
famous formulation 'One day no work, one day no eat.' Born in
Fujian, he succeeded Mázǔ Dàoyi (Ma-tsu Tao-i) as Abbot at
Nankang in Jiangxi, then moved to Xinwu, also in Jiangxi, under
Baizhang Mountain.

BODHIDHARMA A Buddhist monk of the sixth century AD, born in
southern India, who immigrated to China after his ordination.
There, under his Chinese name, Dámó ('Penetrating Finger'), he
came to be revered as the father of the Zen tradition.

DANXIÁ ZǏCHÚN (Tan-hsia Tzu-ch'un, c. 1065 – c. 1135) A Zen
monk whose poems are gathered in the Xutáng Jí – a book whose
title might be translated either Gathering in the Empty Room or
The Vacant Hall Collection. His chosen name, Danxiá, means
Redcloud.

HAKUIN (1685–1768) A Rinzai master, born at Haramachi, near
Mt Fuji. In 1716 he settled in to teach at Shoinji, not far from his
birthplace.

HÁN SHAN (c. 800 AD) The hermit poet of Cold Mountain, in the
Tiantai Range, Zhejiang.

HÓNG ZÌCHÉNG (Hung Tzu-ch'eng, c. 1550–1620) Also called
Hóng Yingmíng (Hung Ying-ming), author of the Caìgen Tán or
Conversations with Vegetable Roots.

JAKUSHITSU GENKO (1290–1367) A Zen monk trained under
Issan. He studied in China from 1320 to 1326 and lived as a
hermit in Okayama, in southwestern Honshu, on his return to
Japan.

JÍZÀNG (Chi-tsang, 549–623) A metaphysician in the tradition of Nagarjuna and Kumarajiva, born in Nanjing. His mother was Chinese, his father Parthian, from what is now northern Afghanistan.

KARAMATSU The name, in Japanese, means 'Chinese pine,' but it is really the Japanese larch, *Larix leptolepis*.

KUMARAJIVA (344–413) A Turkestani scholar from Kucha, under Tien Shan, on the northern rim of the Takla Makan. In 384, when Kucha was invaded by the Chinese, he was taken to Gucang, in Gansu, and in 401 to Chang'an (now Xi'an, in Shaanxi). There the reigning prince installed him in an academy (The Park of Perfect Happiness) where he was free to teach, but which he was not permitted to leave. He translated a number of Buddhist texts from Sanskrit into Chinese and taught several devoted students, including Sengzhaò. To his Chinese students, he was known as Jiumólóshí, 'Dove Caught in the Soldier's Net.'

LARIX LYALLII The alpine larch, a deciduous conifer found only in the Northern Rockies and Cascades.

LÍNJÌ YÌXUÁN (Lin-chi I-hsuan, c. 800–867) A Zen master from Hebei, founder of the monastic tradition which bears his name. In Japan, where the tradition flourished for centuries, he and his school are known as Rinzai.

JOSEF MENGELE (1911–1979?) The German physician in charge of medical experiments at Auschwitz-Birkenau. After the war, he was rumored to be living in South America, then to have drowned near São Paulo. In 1985 a skeleton said to be his was exhumed and its identity exhaustively tested.

NAGARJUNA 'The Serpent Prince,' a Buddhist metaphysician of the second or third century AD, now honored as the principal dialectician of the Madhyamika or 'Middle Way' school of Buddhist thought. He taught near Amaravati, on the Krishna River, in Andhra Pradesh.

NÁNQUÁN PǓYUÀN (Nan-ch'uan P'u-yuan, 738–834) A Zen monk trained, like Baǐzhàng, under 'The Old Horse,' Mázǔ Daòyi, in Jiangxi. His own hermitage was farther north, in the oak forests of Anhui.

PARŚVANATHA   (c. 820–776 BC?) A North Indian sage, tradition-
ally counted the 23rd Patriarch of the Jains.

SARAHA   A Buddhist philosopher-poet living in Bengal and writing
in Apabhramśa, perhaps in the eighth century AD.

SENGZHAÒ   (Seng-chao, 384–414) A Buddhist metaphysician,
born in Shaanxi. He went to Gansu, reputedly at the age of 14, to
study with Kumarajiva. In 401, he returned with his teacher to
Chang'an, where he studied and taught at the academy until his
death at the age of 31.

SHAKUHACHI   An end-blown bamboo flute.

SUGI   The Japanese redwood, *Cryptomeria japonica*.

UDDALAKA ARUNI   One of the legendary sages of India. He speaks
at length in the Chandogya Upanishad.

WÁNG BÌ   (226–249) Precocious author of a commentary on the
works of Lao Tzu. He was a native of Shandong, employed at
Luoyang, the capital of Wei, in what is now northern Henan.

BEN WEBSTER   One of the great tenor sax men. Born in Kansas City
in 1909, he died lonely and cheerless in Amsterdam in 1973.

The following table gives the page number, roman transcription and literal translation of each Chinese or Japanese phrase which appears in the book in ideographic form. The Pinyin system is used to transcribe the Chinese, and the characters are translated word-for-word in sequence, no matter how clumsy may be the resulting English phrase.

3 xiè yǎn tí zì = *Tse Yim inscription character*

9 dà yin xi sheng = *large sound scarce hear*

12 rén shèng = *person holy*

14 banruò boluómìduo = *Sanskrit* prajñā pāramitā, *'transcendent wisdom'*

18 tian dì zhi xin = *sky earth their mindheart*

20 shèng xin míng jí = *holy mindheart dark silent*

22 dámó = *penetrating finger or intelligent touch*

24 èr dì = *double truth*

26 wù wǒ tóng gen = *things I same root*

28 shì fei yi qì = *yes no one breath*

30 yi rì bù zuò / yi rì bù shí = *one day no work, one day no eat*

32 hán shan lù bù daò = *Cold Mountain reach no road*

34 rú shuǐ zhong yuè = *like water within-it moon*

38 yi jiàn guò qing tian = *one arrow outdistance blue sky*

40 xu táng jí = *empty hall assemble*

42 xin dì gan jìng fang kě / dú shu xué gǔ = *mindheart place dry clear before can study book, understand ancients*

46 wú xin sì qiu yuè = *own mindheart similar autumn moon*

48 xin qiaò = *mindheart pierce*

79 nihon-no aoi yane = *Japan its blue roofs*

97 teisho-to sanzen = *lecture and interview*

'Saraha' was first published as a broadside by the King Library Press, Lexington, Kentucky, in 1984. *Tending the Fire* was printed by Glenn Goluska and issued as a chapbook by the Alcuin Society, Vancouver, in 1985. *The Blue Roofs of Japan* had its first performance at the University of Montana, Missoula, on October 16, 1985, and was later broadcast on CBC Radio in a version produced by Don Mowatt. The score was published in 1986 by Jan & Crispin Elsted at Barbarian Press and in a separate edition issued by William Hoffer. 'Thin Man Washing' and 'Absence of the Heart' are reprinted from *The Beauty of the Weapons* (McClelland & Stewart, 1982; Copper Canyon Press, 1985), where they appeared as 'Two Variations.' Several of the other poems first appeared in *The Canadian Forum, Canadian Literature, Cutbank* (Missoula), *Landfall* (Christchurch), *Rambling Jack* (Auckland), *Lines Review* (Edinburgh), *New Orleans Review, The Paris Review* (New York), *Rubicon* (Montreal), *Verse* (Oxford) and *Prism International* (Vancouver). The language reaches everywhere and nowhere, touching everything and nothing – the pages ceasing to be footsteps and becoming merely mouths. 'Breathing through the Feet' first appeared in a more primitive form in the Poets & Politics issue of *Canadian Literature* (Vancouver, 1985) and in its present state in *Margin* (London, 1986)

I am deeply grateful to Bill New and Laurie Ricou for their willingness to listen, to Audrey Thomas for her presence in Japan, and to the Rabbit for the dogged gardening. And I am grateful to the friends whose contributions to the printed book are plainly to be seen: to Vic Marks and his staff at The Typeworks, and to Yim Tse, whose brush, like Baĭzhàng's mind, can think and laugh at once.

The dedication, on page 5, says in Ojibwa *nidodemak kaye dokikinohamakemak*, and in Cree *nitudemak nesta kakiskinohamakecik oci*. These statements translate one another, as they do the English words *for my friends and teachers*.

Bowen Island □ 1986

Printed in the USA
CPSIA information can be obtained
at www.ICGtesting.com
JSHW020051290723
45417JS00001B/3